MAHATMA GANDHI

A Life From Beginning to End

Copyright © 2017 by Hourly History.

All rights reserved.

Table of Contents

Introduction
Growing up in India
Studying Law in London
Political Activism in South Africa
Becoming the Mahatma
The Battle for Independence in India
The Quit India Movement during World War II
Partition and Pakistan
The Martyr of India, the Sage of the Twentieth Century

Introduction

History is filled with unlikely heroes, and the child who was born on October 2, 1869, in India to a local politician and his fourth wife would rank among those who, it seemed, were destined to be ordinary. But in India, October 2 is now a holiday as the nation celebrates the birth of the man who led his country to freedom. Of course, not only was the birth of Mohandas Karamchand Gandhi unlikely to have been an indication of greatness but as India itself had been under British rule for centuries, the juxtaposition of that birth with Indian independence would have been inconceivable when he was born.

Mohandas K. Gandhi, the Mahatma, the father of Indian independence, remains an enigma despite the fact that virtually everyone knows who he was. He grew up in a household with a politically active father and a religiously devout mother, but as a child, he displayed no particular brilliance. He went to school and gave no indication of academic promise. He studied law in England, did well, and returned to India where his law practice eventually failed. When he accepted a job in South Africa, it was because he had no other prospects.

But it was in South Africa that the politics and religion of his upbringing blended together to transform him into a charismatic leader who supported the oppressed and the downtrodden. It was, in fact, in South Africa where he learned that, although he considered himself a citizen of the British Empire, the color of his skin meant that, to those in power, he was a second-class member of society.

Refusing to accept this, Gandhi labored for over 20 years to bring justice to the Indian community in South Africa. And when he returned home, he did so as a political leader determined to fight for independence from Great Britain with the most unlikely weapon of all: nonviolence. Arrested and imprisoned numerous times, Gandhi was not defeated by the punishment that the authorities inflicted upon him because his lifestyle embraced asceticism and self-discipline. What could prison do to a man who fasted and prayed and was so committed to his beliefs that he would not strike out at his enemies?

But for all of Gandhi's successes, he did not get the united India that he wanted; the partitioning of the country into Hindu India and Muslim Pakistan was a grave disappointment to Gandhi, who treasured religious tolerance and diversity and wanted his nation to mirror the spiritual culture he sought. After his assassination, others took up the banner of nonviolent protest that he employed, bringing freedom to the downtrodden and justice to the subjugated.

Gandhi's legacy has influenced countries and individuals far distant in time and geography from India. In 2009, American President Barack Obama, when asked to name the one person he would choose to dine with, named Mohandas Gandhi. "He's somebody I find a lot of inspiration in. He inspired Dr. King with his message of nonviolence. He ended up doing so much and changed the world just by the power of his ethics."

Chapter One

Growing up in India

"Only this much I knew—that under ideal conditions, true education could be imparted only by the parents, and that then there should be the minimum of outside help."

—Mohandas K. Gandhi

He was the youngest child born to Putlibai and Karamchand Uttamchand Gandhi, merchant caste Hindus who lived in Porbandar, a town on the coast of the Kathiawar Peninsula in western India. His father's previous three wives had been disappointments in terms of their childbearing; the first two wives died young, and his third wife was childless. That wife gave him permission to remarry and the fourth time proved to be the charm. Putlibai, who was 13 years old when she married Karamchand Gandhi in 1857, gave birth to two sons and a daughter before Mohandas, the youngest, was born.

Gandhi's father, despite his lack of education, was a man of ability who worked as a prime minister to several different Indian princes. Karamchand, having only gone as far as elementary school, was said by Gandhi to have had no education except for experience. His mother was illiterate, but her piety would have a profound effect on her youngest son's philosophical development. She followed a form of Hinduism which was influenced by Jainism, a theology that emphasized asceticism and nonviolence and the belief that all living creatures were precious and violence should not be done to any of them, no matter how insignificant they seemed to be in comparison to human beings. She prayed often, fasted frequently, and adhered resolutely to her spiritual vows.

Even though her religious discipline was to have a significant effect on her son in later years, when he was young, he found religion dull and uninspiring. The elaborate Hindu temples struck him as excessive, and Gandhi admitted in later years that, as a child, he had leaned toward atheism.

But he grew up in a region where religion was a vigorous influence upon people's lives. Jainism was especially strong in the area where Gandhi was living. His father, Karamchand, was friends with Muslims, Jains, and Parsis, a mixture that inspired religious discussions in the home, and that tolerance in the Gandhi household would remain with him throughout his life.

Gandhi's father was a man of influence, and although the family was not wealthy, they were people of significance in their town. They owned multiple homes in their town as well as in the nearby cities of Rajkot and Kutiana. Gandhi grew up with a nurse to care for him, and he received a good education.

Rajkot was not merely a place where the Gandhis had another home. Gandhi was just five years old when his father became a counselor to the ruler of the Indian state of Rajkot. Although the town was less significant than Porbandar, Rajkot did have the advantage of having a British agency located there. As the son of a man of influence in the area and a mother of strong religious beliefs, Gandhi's childhood was the foundation for his future political and religious convictions which would guide his actions.

Gandhi began his education at the age of nine years old, studying arithmetic, history, and geography. As a child, he was physically unimpressive, too short and slender to be an athlete, and too timid and shy to make an impression on his teachers. He had difficulty learning the multiplication tables; academically and socially, Gandhi was not a brilliant student.

Two years later, he was a high school student and not a particularly impressive one, although his lack of prowess might have been influenced by his extreme shyness. But even a shy boy is not immune to the vicissitudes of adolescence, and that was the case with Gandhi as well. Gandhi experimented with the forbidden taboos of eating meat, smoking, and even petty theft when he stole coins from his servant to purchase cigarettes. When he stole from his brother in order to pay a debt, Gandhi was remorseful and confessed his sin to his father. His father forgave him, but the act changed Gandhi who said that after that episode, telling the truth became his passion.

Introduced by his older brother to a friend who was a bit more worldly, particularly given his Muslim beliefs, the friend took Gandhi to a brothel. However, Gandhi was uncomfortable in the brothel, and the boldness of the prostitutes made him uneasy. The prostitutes weren't any more pleased than he was, and he was ordered out of the brothel. He stopped seeing his brother's friend, who had also proposed that Gandhi should try to grow taller by eating meat, something which the vegetarian youth was opposed to doing.

The traditional view has long been that marriage settles a man down. Gandhi was only 13, but it was not unusual for families to arrange marriages with offspring of that age. The year 1883 was one for family celebrations as marriages were arranged for Gandhi, his brother, and a cousin. Gandhi's 14-year-old bride, Kasturbai Makhanji Kapadia, more familiarly known as Kasturba or Ba, continued to spend much of her time in her family home and not with her in-laws or her one year younger husband. Marriage was a complicated affair for the young teenager, and Gandhi saw marriage as the opportunity to wear new clothes, eat sweets, and play with relatives. In the beginning, the bride and groom were so shy that they barely spoke to one another.

But that dynamic didn't last. Despite his youth, Gandhi had the makings of a demanding husband, and Kasturba was a strong-minded wife. He was jealous when she wanted to spend time with her friends, and when she sought permission to do so, as the custom required, he sometimes refused to allow her. However, his wife disobeyed him and went with her friends anyway. Her rebellion would lead to a quarrel, and husband and wife would spend days not speaking to each other.

It must have been a bewildering experience for the two. Gandhi was still fearful of the dark and couldn't sleep without having a light on in the room, a secret that he didn't reveal to his young wife. But he was a teenage boy, and physical desire for his wife rose powerfully within him. "Even at school, I used to think of her, and the thought of nightfall and our subsequent meeting was ever haunting me," Gandhi recalled.

He was a boy, but he had a strong conscience that afflicted him with remorse for his transgressions. Even the fact that, when he was a child, he had enjoyed twisting the dog's ears troubled him when he recalled this activity as an adult. But there were other memories of his youth that were more soothing to him. He read Indian classics that also left an imprint on him, particularly the stories of Shravana and Harishchandra, which would brand the concepts of truth and love on his impressionable mind, concepts which would later come to remarkable fruition. Harishchandra is the story of an ancient king of India and an honest hero, and Gandhi fell under the story's spell, acting it out to himself countless times as it left its mark upon his imagination. Later, he would seek to bring the values of truth and love to everyday life.

Although his wedding caused him to lose a year of schooling, Gandhi made up the lost time by working harder on his lessons. He graduated from high school in November 1887, but by that time, Gandhi was already both a father and fatherless. Karamchand had died late in 1885 when Gandhi was 16 years old. And unfortunately, the baby born to Gandhi and his wife died only a few days after birth, and the twin tragedies caused the young Gandhi tremendous grief.

With the death of their father, the Gandhi family had less financial security, and his relatives felt that Gandhi could better himself and help his family if he pursued a career. But his entry into college was not a success; he enrolled at Samaldas College which at the time was the only institution granting higher-education degrees in the region. It was also the only school that Gandhi could afford to attend. However, the lectures were dull and failed to stimulate him. After ten days, Gandhi left the college to return home to his family in Porbandar.

A family friend came up with the idea that Gandhi should go to London to study law. His mother and uncle opposed the idea. Gandhi's wife had given birth to a son in July 1888, and the family felt that it was not the time for him to leave, especially to go so far away. His mother also feared that traveling overseas across oceans would cause him to lose his caste, a concern of high-caste Hindus. Despite the opinions of his family and the birth of his son, Gandhi wanted to go. He promised his mother and his wife that while he was in England, he would not indulge in meat, alcohol, or women. He must have been convincing because his mother granted him permission to go, as well as her blessing.

Gandhi began his journey by leaving Porbandar for Bombay, today called Mumbai, staying with the local Modh Bania community as he waited for his travel arrangements to be made. His father had known the head of the community, and the leader was concerned that living in London would lure Gandhi into adopting Western ways and abandoning his religion. Even though Gandhi assured them that he had promised his mother that he would remain faithful to the precepts of his beliefs, the community rejected him. Gandhi did not change his plans despite their dismissal.

He left for London on September 4, 1888, with his brother present to see him off. Dressed in a black suit, a shirt, and a tie, Gandhi was very aware of how different he looked out of his Indian attire. But although he felt that he made an impressive appearance, it was his shyness, more than the unfamiliarity of his garb, that kept him apart from the other passengers. He remained in his cabin while on board the ship, feeding himself with the snacks that he'd brought from home. The food on the ship was unfamiliar to him, and he had vowed to his mother that he would not renege on his vegetarian regimen.

Chapter Two

Studying Law in London

"I must say that, beyond occasionally exposing me to laughter, my constitutional shyness has been no disadvantage whatever. In fact I can see that, on the contrary, it has been all to my advantage. My hesitancy in speech, which was once an annoyance, is now a pleasure. Its greatest benefit has been that it has taught me the economy of words. I have naturally formed the habit of restraining my thoughts. And I can now give myself the certificate that a thoughtless word hardly ever escapes my tongue or pen. I do not recollect ever having had to regret anything in my speech or writing."

—Mohandas K. Gandhi

Gandhi disembarked from the ship at Southampton to see that the variations of Western dress would take some time to understand. The other men were dressed in dark clothing, wearing bowler hats and carrying overcoats, while he was wearing white flannels. It was an embarrassing introduction to the country that would be his home for the next three years, and Gandhi's first impulse was to assimilate into the new setting. As an Indian, he belonged to the British Empire, and he intended to become British.

When he was met by a family friend who was wearing a silk top hat, Gandhi reached out to touch the silk. The friend told him that Westerners did not touch each other's possessions out of respect for one another's privacy and space. He also advised Gandhi to speak in a quiet voice and not to ask too many questions which would be regarded as intrusive. This was Gandhi's first lesson in how to become British.

But the newcomer had to find his own path to the British way of living. For Gandhi, the first challenge was fitting into his new surroundings which were vastly different from India. He started with his appearance; when he bought a top hat and a tie, he studied his reflection in the mirror to try to get everything right, from parting his hair to tying his tie. His attempt to learn to dance didn't fare well and he gave it up, lacking a sense of musical rhythm. French classes and elocution lessons bored him. The violin lessons didn't last long. For three months, he tried to turn himself into an Englishman.

But Gandhi wasn't an Englishman. When he realized that he could not become something he wasn't, Gandhi decided to become what he could be: a scholar. He told a friend, "I have changed my way of life. All this foolishness is at an end. I am living in one room and cooking my own food. Hereafter I shall devote all my time to study."

Instead of paying for transport to reach his destinations, Gandhi walked wherever he needed to go. He began to keep accounts of the money he spent. Mindful of his vow to his mother to remain faithful to his upbringing, Gandhi continued with his vegetarian diet, but the menus offered in British dining were tasteless. His landlady offered to prepare vegetarian food for him, but the meals left him hungry. Fortunately, Gandhi discovered one of London's vegetarian restaurants. He furthered his commitment to vegetarianism by joining the Vegetarian Society where he was elected to the executive committee and wrote articles for the *Vegetarian*.

Members of the Vegetarian Society shared some of Gandhi's ideals and belonged to an organization known as the Theosophical Society which promoted universal brotherhood and Hindu and Buddhist literature. Gandhi joined the group in reading the *Bhagavad Gita*.

Gandhi had come a long way from being the average student of his youth. Dedicating himself to the hard work that was entailed by appearing for the London matriculation examination, Gandhi passed his French, English and chemistry classes; he failed Latin, but when he tried a second time, he passed.

Studying for a legal career was less onerous than it is today. There were a total of approximately 24 dinners in a term, and keeping terms meant attending at least six of them, although the dining was not necessarily the main purpose of the gathering. It was being present that counted, and keeping terms and passing examinations constituted the main curriculum of being called to the bar.

Dining for Gandhi was not as simple as it was for the other law students. Gandhi, who abstained from meat and alcohol, was fearful that he would be teased for his simple food choices, but he was surprised and pleased to learn that refusing meat and wine did not arouse hostility or contempt. Upon seeing Gandhi bring his law books with him when he came to the dinner, his fellow students suggested that instead of reading Roman law in Latin, he should use a translation which would be easier, but Gandhi explained that he enjoyed the completeness of the learning process and liked the harder version.

The more difficult choice of study suited him, and when he took the final examination, he passed with high grades and was called to the bar on June 10, 1891, as a barrister and enrolled in the High Court the following day. It seemed that he was well on his way to success.

No one could have predicted that, in 1922, the Honourable Society of the Inner Temple would disbar Mohandas Karamchand Gandhi and strike his name from the rolls. By that time, Gandhi had been convicted of sedition, and the man who had once tried so hard to act and look like an Englishman was redefining the identity of Indians as he led their fight for independence. Gandhi's name was not reinstated in the Inner Temple until 1988.

But the future was not yet written. And after three years in England, Gandhi set sail for home on June 12, 1891. The experience had been rewarding, and Gandhi felt that after India, England was the place he would most want to live. But when he returned home, India was not as he had left it. When he arrived, he learned that his family had kept the news of his mother's death from him.

The family still had great hopes that with Gandhi's education and English experience, they would all prosper. However, Gandhi discovered that his education had failed to provide him with a complete knowledge of the law and, following the advice of friends, he went to Bombay to study Indian law so that he could establish himself as a barrister.

But the law, it seemed, had served him better as an educational effort than as a means of earning a living. His law practice failed. He tried to get a part-time job teaching high school but was rejected. Finally, he had no choice but to go back to Rajkot and earn his living by drafting petitions for litigants. This business failed too.

With failure behind him and few options lined up, Gandhi was offered a position in South Africa for an Indian firm, Dada Abdulla & Company. It was in this set of circumstances that, in April 1893, he accepted a year-long contract to a post in the colony of Natal, South Africa. The company wanted a native of Kathiawar to do the work, and Gandhi would be paid travel expenses and £105 a year. Gandhi accepted the offer, and he, his wife, and three children left India for this other outpost in the British Empire. Expecting to be there only until the end of his 12-month contract, Gandhi ended up staying for more than 20 years and during that time, the evolution of the Mahatma would begin.

Chapter Three
Political Activism in South Africa

> *"It was only in South Africa that I got over this shyness, though I never completely overcame it. It was impossible for me to speak impromptu. I hesitated whenever I had to face strange audiences and avoided making a speech whenever I could. Even today I do not think I could or would even be inclined to keep a meeting of friends engaged in idle talk."*
>
> —Mohandas K. Gandhi

The British Empire extended far beyond the European island of Great Britain. When Gandhi arrived in Natal, South Africa in 1893, he regarded himself as British first and Indian second. That ranking would undergo a transformation that would change how he felt about his citizenship, and then how he saw India's role in the Empire.

His instruction in the different tiers of Britishness began right away. In a courtroom in Durban, a magistrate ordered him to remove his turban. Gandhi refused. And it was a train ride to Pretoria that forged his consciousness of the lurking discrimination that was as much a caste system of the British as anything he had known in India.

During the train ride, Gandhi was beaten by a white driver because he insisted on keeping his seat instead of giving it up to a white person and taking a seat on the floor. He spent the night in the train station, wondering if he should return to India or stay in South Africa.

He stayed. When he tried to board the train the following day, there were no problems, at least on the train. But South Africa was a minefield of episodes that opened Gandhi's eyes. A police officer once kicked him off a path and into the street because Indians were not allowed to walk on the public footpaths in South Africa.

After finishing the legal work that he had traveled to South Africa to do in 1894, the Indian community gathered to bid him farewell before he went back home. But instead of returning to India, Gandhi, responding to new government legislation that was discriminatory, decided to stay and help the Indians oppose a bill that would have denied them the right to vote because voting was believed to be something reserved for Europeans. Gandhi helped found the Natal Indian Congress in 1894 and with an organizational foundation upon which to stand, the Indians in South Africa were forged into a political group.

Gandhi's work on behalf of equal rights for people of color did not win him acclaim among the white community. He was attacked by a mob of whites when he arrived in Durban in 1897, luckily the wife of the police superintendent was able to help him escape. Gandhi, however, would not press charges against his attackers.

Gandhi was not only combatting the political reality of what it was like to be a person of color in a society where white skin indicated power and superiority. He was also fighting against stereotypes and misperceptions. Knowing that, according to the British way of thinking, Hindus were effete and unable to participate in vigorous or adventurous activities, Gandhi challenged that myth in 1900 during the Boer War by forming the Natal Indian Ambulance Corps. He raised a total of 1,100 volunteers who received training and medical certification so that they could support the British soldiers fighting the Boers on the front lines.

It wasn't a sit-on-the-sidelines task. At Spion Kop, the stretcher-bearers were on the front lines, carrying wounded British soldiers on foot because the ambulances weren't able to handle the terrain. They had to walk for miles to get the soldiers to a field hospital, and for their heroism, Gandhi and 37 other Indians were awarded the Queen's South Africa Medal.

His political consciousness awakened, Gandhi noticed that the people he thought of as fellow British citizens had a sense of superiority toward other citizens of the Empire because of their skin color or background. He knew that he was not the only one to experience the bigotry; there was an entire country of people just like him who had believed themselves to be equal partners in the Empire and, as Gandhi was discovering, that was not how they were viewed.

The Boer War ended, but the racism was an ingrained part of the South African social framework. And in 1906, the South African government ordered the Indians and Chinese in the colony to register.

Gandhi's premise was that the law should be defied and the ones opposing it should accept the inevitable punishment that would accompany their acts. He did not yet conceive of his evolving protest movement as a political direction, but as the discrimination continued, Gandhi realized that treating people with cruelty because of their skin color was morally wrong. All people had rights, and those rights had to be observed.

Gandhi was an Indian, and his focus was on the racism that Indians were experiencing. He had not yet come to adopt a global view of civil rights, and the harsh treatment that Africans received in South Africa was not something he was protesting at this time. But he was a young man, and when preparing a legal brief in 1895 for the Natal Assembly to seek the right to vote for Indians, he argued that Indians should not be categorized in the same group as Africans because both Anglo-Saxons and Indians came from the Indo-European demographic.

His views on racism would evolve the more he dedicated himself to the struggle for rights for Indians, but it was an evolution and not an epiphany. In decades to come, a South African leader would follow the path set by Gandhi, as Nelson Mandela adopted the practice of civil disobedience to bring freedom against the apartheid government of his country. But that was many years away, and Gandhi was laboring in a time when racism was tolerated by civilizations all over the globe.

When Great Britain went to war again in 1906, Gandhi once again organized a volunteer group of Indians to serve as an ambulance unit. But this time, his volunteers took care not only of the British who were wounded but also the wounded warriors of the opposing Zulu Kingdom, against whom the British were fighting. Gandhi realized that by taking part in the ambulance unit, the Indians could reshape negative opinions that many British held against people whose skin was dark.

His campaign, however, was not admired by the white soldiers, and they tried to prevent him from taking care of the wounded Zulus; some of the stretcher bearers were shot and killed. Gandhi was beginning to realize that, far from being a beacon of enlightenment, Westerners held staunchly racist views against people who looked different from the way they looked.

Gandhi's campaign against the South African government's discrimination toward Indians, which began in 1906, would last eight years, and hundreds of Indians who lived in South Africa would end up in jail. Indian miners who went on strike were flogged, sent to prison, and sometimes shot. But their resistance paid off, and finally, pressured by the governments of Great Britain and India, South Africa conceded defeat. Indian marriages were recognized, and the poll tax on Indians was abolished. The failed barrister had won a victory that surpassed anything he could have achieved in a courtroom.

Chapter Four
Becoming the Mahatma

"An earthquake, a sort of general upheaval on the political plane—the Government ceases to function . . . the police stations, the courts, offices, etc., all cease to be Government property and shall be taken charge of by the people."

—Mohandas K. Gandhi

When Gandhi returned to India in 1915 after more than 20 years in South Africa, he came home with a reputation as an Indian nationalist. The citizens of Bombay honored him upon his arrival with a reception, and the Indian government bestowed upon him a Kaiser-i-Hind Medal in the King's 1915 Birthday Honours list.

His accomplishments in South Africa, although in defiance of the laws of that country, were not perceived as anything that would spread the fever of rebellion to India. There had even been support among influential Britons for Gandhi's pursuit of justice. But Gandhi had learned that the discrimination he had witnessed in South Africa was not unique to the African continent. Such a stance was destined to bring him into conflict with the Brits. There was already an organized Indian political movement thriving in the country, following Gokhale, a leader of the Indian National Congress Party who believed in working for change from within rather than upsetting the status quo. But Gandhi, as he would soon demonstrate, had not come back home to protect the status quo for Great Britain.

Just as India was changing, so was Great Britain, which was locked in battle against the Germans in the First World War, a conflict that would bring cataclysmic change to the ruling families of Europe. Gandhi supported the British in their fight against the Germans but was critical of the colonial imperialism that treated native peoples unjustly. However, he agreed to recruit Indians to fight in this war and not to serve as an ambulance unit as he had done in past British conflicts. The discrepancy between his belief in nonviolence or Ahimsa and the campaign to recruit soldiers did not go unnoticed.

His support of the war effort did not mean that he abandoned his crusade on behalf of Indians. Realizing that independence from the British would require more than oratory, Gandhi believed that his country needed to achieve economic independence first. He promoted the manufacturing of homespun cloth to replace the textiles that were imported from the British.

The year 1917 saw World War I still raging, but in India, Gandhi's battle of protesting by nonviolent means achieved its first victory. The peasants of Champaran were forced to grow indigo as a cash crop, but demand for indigo had been dropping. The indigo growers made their case to Gandhi. As Gandhi's political influence had grown, his spiritual reputation had also matured. He was admired for his simple way of living; his reliance on prayer, meditation and fasting won him the title of Mahatma, or "great-souled one," from his admirers. He also had considerable political clout with the backing of the Indian National Congress. To everyone's surprise, the nonviolent protest movement was successful, and the indigo planters were able to wrest concessions from the authorities.

The following year, when floods and famine struck the town of Kheda, Gandhi supported the local residents in their demand for tax relief. His noncooperation tactics led to a signature campaign: the peasants pledged that they would not pay the revenue even if their land was confiscated. The local revenue officials were socially boycotted. It took five months, but by May 1918, the government eased the requirement to pay the taxes until the famine had ended.

Aware that the end of World War I had not solved its internal problems, the government decided that dissent needed to be controlled. When Parliament passed the Rowlatt Acts in March 1919, giving the colonial authorities the powers to suppress activities that were deemed as subversive, Gandhi responded by setting up a campaign of passive resistance. The British were alarmed at the growing unrest in India, and extending the measures of the Defence of India Regulations Act that had been put into place during World War I seemed an expedient way to maintain control. Anyone suspected of acting against the British authorities could be imprisoned without trial.

Indian political leaders were outraged that punishment could be so liberally meted out, and as a result, the Rowlatt Satyagraha went into effect. Indians were called upon to fast and suspend all business to demonstrate their opposition to the new law. But by the end of March, there was rioting in the provinces. On April 10, two Indian leaders were arrested and their location was not divulged. On April 13, nearly 400 Indians in attendance at a peaceful protest at Amritsar were slaughtered by soldiers firing over 1,600 rounds of ammunition into the crowd without warning. A doctor on the scene estimated the number of dead or wounded at over 1,500.

Gandhi temporarily suspended the resistance campaign. He felt that Indians were not yet ready to behave in harmony with the nonviolent principles of Ahimsa. He also felt that the government of India was deaf to the outcries of the Indians it was supposed to represent.

On behalf of the Indian National Congress, Gandhi was invested with executive authority in December 1921, and the Congress Party was galvanized. With reorganization and a new constitution, it was no longer necessary to pay a fee to join, and that transformed the organization from an exclusive group into one that was designed to appeal to the masses.

Gandhi continued to pursue his program of economic independence, urging Indians to wear homespun cloth rather than British imports and to boycott goods that were made elsewhere. He also expected Indians, whether they were wealthy or poor, to spend some time daily spinning the cloth, known as khadi, to demonstrate their support for the independence movement. His purpose was to nurture a sense of discipline and dedication to the movement as well as to grant women a political role in the struggle. The boycotting expanded to include not only the products that were made in Great Britain but also the courts of law, educational institutions, and government employment, as well as returning titles and honors that had been granted by the British government.

Although Gandhi planned to proceed with caution, his goal was mass civil disobedience so that the institutions controlled by the British and denied to Indians would eventually be taken over by the Indians. By launching civil disobedience in one district and gauging its success, it would then be brought to nearby areas until finally, all of India was liberated by the contagious effects of nonviolent protest. He stressed the need to keep the movement nonviolent so that the independence movement was characterized as a peaceful one.

A new decade had dawned and with it a new leader, who was perceived as central to the Indian independence movement, with methods that did not rely on strength or guns, but on something that almost seemed ludicrous: nonviolent protest to achieve self-government.

Chapter Five

The Battle for Independence in India

"I want world sympathy in this battle of Right against Might."

—Mohandas K. Gandhi

The British, of course, had no intention of aiding Gandhi in his dream of Swaraj or self-government. They were willing to offer reforms, albeit on a minor level, but not independence. The Rowlatt Acts, with the intention of imprisoning anyone accused of subversive acts, also intended to punish Gandhi's civil disobedience tactics by treating members of the movement as terrorists.

On March 10, 1922, Gandhi was arrested and charged with sedition; he pleaded guilty and was sentenced to six years in prison. Deprived of his leadership, the Indian National Congress divided into two factions; one group supported participation in the existing legislature and the other opposed. Fissures in the Indian population began to show as well. The dissension between the Muslims and the Hindus erupted in response to actions by the dynamic Turkish leader Ataturk and the collapse of a Turkish caliphate. In response, Muslim Indians left the Congress Party to form their own organizations.

After two years in prison, Gandhi was released in 1924 to undergo an operation for appendicitis. If the British hoped that Gandhi would limit his political activism following his release, they were wrong. In 1928, at the Calcutta Congress, Gandhi supported a resolution that called on the British to grant dominion status to India. The alternative would be a renewed campaign of noncooperation. His proposal was rejected. And so, the Indian National Congress decided to celebrate the nation's Independence Day on January 26, 1930, with other Indian organizations joining in the Congress Party's celebration. The participating members took a pledge of independence, vowing that India would one day be free from its shackles.

Independence was a call to a new Satyagraha as Gandhi led the protests against the tax on salt. Thousands of Indians marched with Gandhi from March 12 to April 6, from Ahmedabad to Dandi where he intended to produce salt and not pay the tax. Women as well as men marched, and Gandhi welcomed them as political activists in this campaign. Approximately 100,000 people set out with him on the 240-mile journey.

As the marchers passed through the villages, the protest also became a political organizing activity as donations were collected, new adherents to Satyagraha were signed up, and village officials resigned from their offices rather than cooperate with the British. Gandhi was interviewed by the press and even the foreign media were intrigued; *The New York Times* reported almost daily on the progress of the marchers, and when the march ended, it was a front-page story.

Each evening, the marchers stopped in a village along the route, and Gandhi requested a place to spend the night, a place to wash, and food. The end of the march signified a violation of the salt laws, and Gandhi, along with over 80,000 other Indians, was arrested. The Indians were energized as even poor members felt included in the battle against the salt tax that Gandhi called inhuman. But the British were stubborn.

Gandhi's incarceration did not halt the Salt Satyagraha. A planned raid on the salt depots at Dharasana went on as scheduled, with 2,500 participants. They began the raid with prayer and a reminder to remain faithful to nonviolence. When they advanced to the depot, they were ordered to disperse by the police. They said nothing but continued to move forward, even as the policemen beat them. An American reporter who witnessed the scene wrote, "In eighteen years of reporting in twenty-two countries, I have never witnessed such harrowing scenes as at Dharasana. Sometimes the scenes were so painful that I had to turn away momentarily."

Realizing that Gandhi's influence over the Indian people was unlikely to wane, the British viceroy, Lord Irwin, was open to negotiations. In March 1931, the Gandhi-Irwin Pact was signed; in exchange for the suspension of his civil disobedience campaign, all of India's political prisoners would be freed. Gandhi was invited to London as the representative of the Indian

National Congress. Unfortunately, the discussions failed to discuss the transfer of power that the Congress sought.

Determined to hold onto India, British politicians including Winston Churchill denigrated Gandhi and his methods. Churchill called him a "seditious Middle Temple lawyer" and a fakir who chose to appear half-naked to negotiate as an equal with the representatives of the British king. Churchill's words revealed the mindset of the British and their obliviousness to the authentic leadership of Gandhi. At another of the conferences, the British challenged the authority of Gandhi and the Congress Party to speak for all of India, including the Muslims and Sikhs. Gandhi resisted the proposal to create a constitution that was based upon the division in the country and would serve to create deeper divisions while distracting attention away from the overriding intention to free India from colonial domination.

In 1931, after British authorities made some concessions, Gandhi again called off the resistance movement and agreed to represent the Congress Party at the Round Table Conference in London. Meanwhile, some of his party colleagues—particularly Muhammed Ali Jinnah, a leading voice for India's Muslim minority—grew frustrated with Gandhi's methods and what they saw as an absence of actual gains.

Gandhi was aware of the divisions in Indian society even among Hindus. When he returned from London, Gandhi went on a hunger strike to protest the treatment of the untouchable caste. His supporters rallied, and the Hindu government quickly moved to establish reforms.

But the Congress Party seemed to be losing its connection to the people. Seeking a new approach to invigorate the effectiveness of the Congress Party, and give a greater voice to the diverse members who belonged to it, Gandhi resigned from the Indian Congress Party in 1934.

There were other reasons for his resignation. There had been three recent attempts to assassinate him. He also had a new cause to focus on: the work of the villagers. People in the village worked long and hard, unnoticed by the government or the media. Their lot was an unglamorous one, and there was no ulterior motive on Gandhi's part as he set out to help. But when Gandhi turned his attention to their plight, the suspicion was that he planned to use this effort to spread rebellion in the rural areas. Provincial governments were told to watch out for signs of unrest.

Gandhi was not out of politics for long, returning to the Congress Party in 1936. He continued to promote his goal of independence for India and justice for Indians. In an effort to urge the ruler of Rajkot to accept democratic reforms, Gandhi went on a fast unto death, taking no food until the reforms were enacted. The country watched in suspense; the people prayed, and business in the bustling cities stalled. When the viceroy agreed to have a council set up to explore ways to initiate democratic means of governing, Gandhi agreed to break his fast by taking a sip of orange juice.

But while Gandhi's attention was focused on India, the rest of the world was being forced to gaze upon a wider stage. Militarism in Germany, Italy, and Japan made the prospect of another global war more likely. The subject of war was by its nature a challenge for Gandhi, but so was the matter of Indian representation in government. When the viceroy of India did not consult the Indian members of the government before joining in the declaration of war against Germany in 1939, the National Congress Party withdrew its support.

Gandhi opposed joining the British in their war against the Axis Powers, but his position was not shared by others as more than 2.5 million Indians joined the military to fight with the British. Once again, the world was at war. But this time, the quest for Indian independence from Great Britain was not a fledgling movement, but an established campaign. Great Britain was no longer the Empire it had been during the First World War. But that didn't mean that the British would surrender India without a fight.

Chapter Six

The Quit India Movement during World War II

"Ours is not a drive for power, but purely a nonviolent fight for India's independence. . . . The power, when it comes, will belong to the people of India, and it will be for them to decide."

—Mohandas K. Gandhi

From Gandhi's perspective, supporting the British in a war that was fought to advance freedom when that very freedom was denied to the Indians under British rule was a violation of justice. He did not support the Nazis or the Fascists, however; his stance was purely concentrated on the truest meaning of freedom and the people who should enjoy it.

In 1942, as the war raged on oceans and continents, Gandhi gave a speech renewing the call for independence. The Quit India Movement was an unambiguous call to action, and the British wasted no time in arresting Gandhi and the members of the Congress working committee. In retaliation, Indians attacked and burned down the railway stations and police stations owned by the government and cut up telegraph lines. Gandhi encouraged noncooperation but not violence; he said that Indians needed to be willing to endure violence if the British inflicted it upon them, but they could not respond in kind. The image of the movement was at stake, and Gandhi was eager for its purity to be maintained.

During the two years of his incarceration, he suffered great personal loss when his wife died in 1944. She had been arrested with Gandhi in 1942 for her participation in the Quit India Movement and was sentenced to the same prison as her husband at the Aga Khan Palace. She had been at his side throughout his activism and was a firm believer in the causes that he represented. Given the times in which they lived, theirs was not a traditional political marriage, but the bond between the two was a strong one.

Kasturba Gandhi had suffered from bronchitis since she was a child and later, as an adult, she had had pneumonia. She had been ailing since two heart attacks confined her to her bed and she had difficulty breathing which made sleeping difficult. When she asked to see a traditional Indian doctor for treatment, the authorities delayed approval. She finally received treatment and improved for a brief time, but then fell ill again and died on February 22, 1944, in her husband's arms.

Gandhi was released from prison in May 1944. He had suffered an attack of malaria and, at age 74, his health was failing. The British government feared how the public would react if Gandhi died in prison and released him before his sentence was served to avoid any potential public outcry. During his time off the political stage, India had changed. With Congress Party leaders in prison, the remaining political groups had strengthened, and not everyone wanted a united India. The Indian Muslims were advocating for a divided India and a Muslim state.

With the war near its end and victory ahead for the Allies, the British indicated that when World War II was over, they would allow the Indians to have the power they sought. With this concession, Gandhi agreed to end the noncooperation campaign and approximately 100,000 political prisoners, including the Congress Party's leaders, were released from prison.

In March 1946, British representatives arrived in India to plan the process for transferring power from Great Britain to India. India would remain a dominion of the British Commonwealth. The Cabinet Mission, as it was called, was made up of the Secretary of State for India, the President of the Board of Trade, and the First Lord of the Admiralty. Meeting with representatives of the Indian National Congress and the All-India Muslim League, which were the two largest political parties in the Indian assembly, the Mission sought to determine how the two factions could share power and decide whether the country should be united or divided.

The Congress Party hoped that they would be able to address the Muslim issue after the British were gone, but the All-India Muslim League, under the leadership of Muhammad Ali Jinnah, wanted safeguards for their political representation. On May 16, 1946, the Cabinet Mission proposed a plan that would create a united Dominion of India with Muslim-majority provinces grouped together and Hindu-majority provinces grouped together.

By the following month, the plan had changed because of the Congress Party's disapproval at grouping Hindu and Muslim majorities in order to balance one another in the legislature. The Muslims distrusted the Congress Party's reluctance to protect their political involvement in the future government, fearing that Hindus would be ruling Muslims.

Unable to find common ground, the June proposal would divide the country. India would be a Hindu-majority country and Pakistan would be created as a Muslim-majority country. On August 14, 1947, and August 15, 1947, respectively, the British would transfer power to the Dominion of Pakistan and the Union of India. The Congress Party's leaders accepted the plan, although Gandhi did not approve of it. He feared that the partition would unleash what he called "mad violence."

It looked as though the Quit India Movement of Gandhi's party and the Divide and Quit India campaign of Jinnah were implacable and could not meet on common ground. Calling for a Direct Action Day on August 16, 1946, Jinnah encouraged Muslims to gather in support of partition, thereby dividing Muslims and non-Muslims.

But Direct Action Day became known as the Great Calcutta Riot, as Calcutta was the scene of rioting and slaughter. Members of the Muslim League attacked Hindus and Sikhs and to retaliate, members and supporters of the Congress Party attacked Muslims.

Within 72 hours, over 4,000 people were killed. The violence spread to the surrounding regions in what was called the Week of the Long Knives. The police had been given the day off as a holiday and weren't present to stop the mayhem, and the British did not send in its military to restore order.

Learning of the violence, Gandhi traveled to the areas where it was taking place, pleading for the people who were responding out of fear and hatred to embrace peace for all. His concerns that the partition of India would erupt in unprecedented violence would prove to be true. The day when India became a free country was destined to be a bloodbath.

Chapter Seven
Partition and Pakistan

"My whole soul rebels against the idea that Hinduism and Islam represent two antagonistic cultures and doctrines. To assent to such a doctrine is for me a denial of God."

—Mohandas K. Gandhi

When August 15, 1947, brought India its long-awaited independence from Great Britain, the architect of the movement spent the day in Calcutta, not celebrating but instead fasting and spinning. As he had feared, the division of the country had unleashed terrible violence, as more than ten million non-Muslims made their way from the newly-created country of Pakistan into India, and as Muslims in India journeyed to Pakistan. Over half a million were killed in the rioting that resulted, and the hostility between the two nations was destined to remain bitter decades later.

Who could have predicted such carnage and hatred between people who, separated by a manufactured boundary and their religious beliefs, would become such entrenched enemies? The long history of Hindus and Muslims had given no indication that with independence from Britain would come spilled blood between two religious groups who had lived together for so long. But the Second World War had ended, and the map, along with the people populating it, was very different now.

Muslims had been in India since the days of thriving trade with Arabia in the ancient world and even before the arrival of Islam, when Arab traders went to the coast of Konkan-Gujarat and the Malabar region and from there to southeast Asian ports. Muslims first settled in India near the end of the seventh century. As Islam began to spread and bring converts, Muslims found a home in southern India where they intermarried with Indian women and developed an Indian-Arabian community.

As centuries passed and the British became dominant in India, there were also Muslim Indians who considered independence against the British. Muslims and Hindus soldiers or sepoys in the military were discriminated against for their styles of dress. When British rules forbade Hindu sepoys from having religious marks on their foreheads and required Muslims to shave their beards and trim their mustaches and no longer wear turbans, the sepoys were outraged. The Vellore Mutiny and better-known Sepoy Mutiny showed that there were times when the British failed to understand the religious identity of the people of India.

Gandhi understood the religious differences between Muslim and Hindu but did not feel that they should divide the population. Gandhi had supported the Ottoman Empire during the war as part of his determination to defeat British imperialism. The Muslims of India appreciated Gandhi's efforts during the First World War to come to the aid of Muslims who had been wounded or imprisoned. There had been friction between the Hindus and Muslims of India for a long time under British rule, but Gandhi envisioned a united India where religious tolerance flourished and where the British were no longer in charge.

Gandhi sought cooperation between Hindus and Muslims in order for the British to be defeated. He gave his support to the Khilafat movement in India, which saw the Turkish Caliph as a symbol of the Sunni Muslim intention to support Islamic law after the Ottomans were brought down. The Indian Hindus opposed any support for the Khilafat movement, and they were suspicious of Gandhi's decision. But the support he showed for the Caliph brought a halt, although a temporary one, to the violence between Hindus and Muslims, demonstrating their unity as they held joint Satyagraha rallies, and making Gandhi the central figure of Indian politics.

The advent of the twentieth century had ushered in an intensification for the independence movement, which claimed Muslim martyrs who were hanged for their efforts to secure freedom from Great Britain. Muhammad Ali Jinnah, who belonged to the Indian National Congress, was dedicated to the fight for independence, along with other Muslims who saw their destiny as a shared battle against the British for a free and united India. Jinnah, who had been a member of the Imperial Legislative Council, resigned after the legislation authorized the imprisonment of Indians who were regarded as subversives. But Jinnah opposed Gandhi's Satyagraha movement, preferring self-government that could be achieved constitutionally. When he spoke out against Satyagraha at the Indian National Congress in 1920 and was shouted down, he resigned from the Congress.

However, by the time that 1922 was drawing to a close, the Khilafat movement had been brought to an end by Ataturk of Turkey. The discord between Indian Muslims and Hindus returned. Muslim support for Gandhi faded. To Gandhi, this divide between Indians of different religions was painful, and in 1924, in an effort to bring accord between the country's Muslims, he fasted for 21 days. But Gandhi's belief in treating Hindus and Muslims in the same manner was not shared by the Hindus, who were accused—not without reason—of treating the Muslims the way the British treated the Hindus.

As the decades went by and the struggle for an independent India went on, the religious animosity between Hindu and Muslim Indians increased. After Gandhi was arrested, along with other leaders of the Congress Party for their role in the Quit India campaign, the political drama continued. Upon his release from prison in 1944, Gandhi found out that Muhammad Ali Jinnah's support for a divided India and the creation of a Muslim state was the prime topic when the subject of an independent India was discussed.

Gandhi had supported a united India with tolerance and diversity as the centerpiece of its culture, not a nation divided by religious boundaries. The horrific massacre that took place in Calcutta on Direct Action Day proved how deeply the religious discord between Muslims and

Hindus had divided the country. The creation of two nations was a solution that may have worked on a map but did nothing to develop the peace for which Gandhi had spent his life fighting.

Chapter Eight

The Martyr of India, the Sage of the Twentieth Century

"Friends and comrades, the light has gone out of our lives, and there is darkness everywhere, and I do not quite know what to tell you or how to say it. Our beloved leader, Bapu as we called him, the father of the nation, is no more."

— Jawaharlal Nehru

Gandhi did not have long to enjoy the independence that he had been instrumental in bringing to India. On January 30, 1948, as he was on his way to a prayer meeting, an assassin fired three bullets at point-blank range, killing the revered leader. The shooter's name was Nathuram Godse, a Hindu nationalist who did not attempt to escape and was arrested on the spot. His collaborators were arrested in the weeks that followed. Godse explained that he regarded Gandhi as responsible for the violence that had taken place during the partition into India and Pakistan. Gandhi, Godse felt, failed to react to the threat of Muslims. Godse was found guilty and executed the following year.

Announcing Gandhi's death, Prime Minister Jawaharlal Nehru mourned the loss of Gandhi's life, but also |mourned the fact that he would no longer be there for India's leaders to go to when seeking his wise advice. "That is a terrible blow," Nehru said, "not only for me, but for millions and millions in this country."

The funeral procession for Gandhi was five miles long, as more than two million mourners lined up to share the nation's grief and to give honor to Gandhi's memory. In accordance with Hindu tradition, Gandhi was cremated, and his ashes were put into urns for memorial services across India.

Even in a tragedy of international significance, as Gandhi's death was, there was political capital to be made and Nehru lost no time in doing so. Hindu nationalism, which had been the cause of Gandhi's assassination, was seen as a weapon of division. The Congress Party called on Indians to honor the legacy of the Mahatma by working for peace and nonviolence. The Congress Party, although it mourned the loss of its long-time leader, was able to garner consolidation and support for its programs and establish its preeminence in politics. Gandhi as a symbol was useful for the Congress Party and for India. The new nation was forging its path after centuries of colonial domination, but they had the benefit of the memory of a strong leader whose commitment to the Indian people was never in doubt.

Nehru said that Gandhi would no longer be available to offer advice and guidance to those who seek it, but his legacy contradicts that statements. In the 1950s and 1960s, in segregated America, Martin Luther King, Jr. called upon the lessons of nonviolent protest to bring civil rights reform for the nation's African-Americans. Toward the end of the twentieth century, Nelson Mandela heeded the Mahatma's call for nonviolence to put a stop to the apartheid rule which had kept black-skinned South Africans subjugated as a second-class race for so long, a state that Gandhi had known firsthand. In terms of peaceful protest, Mahatma Gandhi was the father of the twentieth century.

It was, to be sure, a violent and rapacious century, one which stood out for the hideous evil which people and nations inflicted upon one another. But the work of Gandhi and King and Mandela, and all those who follow his principles of protest through peaceful means, is as much a beacon of the past century as the cruelty and barbarism are its darkness.

Gandhi was a complicated man, not a saint. In his quest for a life of purity, he may have failed the people who were closest to him. He did not allow his sons to have a formal education, depriving them of the means to choose their own way of living. His eldest son, Harilal, was an alcoholic who was arrested for embezzlement. Gandhi eventually disowned this firstborn son, whose life was one of destitution and disgrace. Gandhi occupied a rarefied position in his public life; his children might have preferred a father who was not an icon, but Gandhi's destiny was to father a nation.

He spent his life seeking truth, and his practices and philosophies have proven to be timeless, as downtrodden people have embraced civil disobedience as a way to make their voices heard, to legitimize their cause, and to, ultimately, succeed in their just goals. He empowered people who thought they had no powerful weapons with which to fight, showing them that by enlisting their spiritual strength in a battle to achieve a noble end, they were stronger than an army, mightier than an empire. There is an irony in the fact that the twentieth century, which unleashed the most devastating weapons that human beings had ever used against one another, also nurtured the philosophy that nonviolence would succeed where clubs, bombs, and bullets would ultimately fail.

When *Time Magazine* compiled a list of the people it described as the Children of Gandhi, the names tell the story of countries, causes, and lives that were forever altered by those who, in following the path of the Mahatma, transformed the world: Benigno Aquino, Cesar Chavez, the 14th Dalai Lama, Martin Luther King, Jr., Aung San Suu Kyi, Nelson Mandela, and Desmond Tutu. Gandhi's legacy lives on.

Printed in Great Britain
by Amazon